An Album of Old LYMINGTON and Milford-on-Sea

CHRISTOPHER HOBBY

Ensign
PUBLICATIONS

Published by Ensign Publications
2 Redcar Street, Shirley, Southampton SO1 5LL.

ISBN 185455 020 9

Typesetting and artwork by Robert Antony, Ringwood, Hants.

Jacket front: **LYMINGTON HIGH STREET,** c 1908

Jacket back: **MILFORD MILL,** c 1900

INTRODUCTION

"Thought you would like a postcard of dear little Milford, but alas it's getting modernized and so many of the old friends departed". So wrote a correspondent in 1906, which goes to prove that nostalgia is not something particularly connected to this age. Just as the writer of the card bemoans the passing of the years, this book aims to relive many of the memories of the period from the latter part of the 19th Century when Great Britain was at the height of its power and the Empire was in its heyday. From the passing of Queen Victoria in 1901 through the social Edwardian era, the traumas of the "Great War" and the reign of King George V up to the late 1940's, this publication endeavours to give an insight into life in Lymington and the surrounding areas of Pennington, Everton, Milford-on-Sea and Keyhaven. The photographs show the residents at work, their environment, at play, and the great celebrations in an era where the "old order" was slipping away and life as we know it today was developing.

Lymington by the late 1800s had ceased to be a port of some significance, its wealth no longer coming from the Salt Industry which had made the town so rich and influential during the 18th Century. With cheap salt coming from the opening of the Cheshire salt beds, one by one the salt pans ceased production along the Keyhaven/Pennington marshes. The only reminders of that prosperous age to remain are an aged building in Woodside, a former boiling house, and the indentations in the fields where the pans once lay. Agriculture and seafaring were the major occupations, and all were influenced to a greater or lesser degree by the owners of the larger houses, Walhampton, Pylewell, to name but two, whose estates were vast and the source of much employment.

The year 1900 found Lymington pretty much unchanged, as it had been for several hundred years. Cars were just coming into use, being afforded only by the gentry and well outnumbered by horse drawn transport. Ladies would travel by open Landau to deal with their shopping requirements and it would be unthinkable to commence such an expedition before mid-morning. The shopkeeper would, when bringing items to the carriage, never turn his back on his patron, so walking backwards became a cultivated art! Such society would never dream of buying items with cash; everything was always on account. The poor trader not only had to deliver the goods but had to wait up to three months for his money.

The market was not as we know it today. The stallholders set up in the afternoon but most of their trade was done in the evening, the High Street being lit by acetylene lamps. The market stalls were as popular then as now. In the evening the traffic could not move freely with locals and visitors strolling down the street viewing the stalls, and, from the 1920s, many enjoying their fish and chips from E. Wilkins' mobile shop which was usually stationed outside the "Anchor and Hope".

Shops were very much specialized, not only in their trades but also to the social level of their clientele. Thus Bennett & Sons, drapers of 110 High Street catered for the local working classes, whilst G. Elliott & Son's firm was well regarded amongst the upper classes.

People had to make their own entertainment, in their homes or in the public houses. Those who wished to extend their knowledge (and had the money) could become members of the Literary Institute in New Lane since the 1840s and rebuilt in 1897. The Assembly Rooms at 109, High Street provided entertainment in the form of the Electric Palace run by Messrs Elgar and Barnard. However, on Monday 22nd December, 1913, the Lyric in St. Thomas Street opened its doors to the public. What was to be the area's main cinema had a very unhappy start as the impressive building was found to have a major structural weakness as its steel trusses were insufficient to carry the roof. After only nine weeks of trade the building was closed for repair, its operating profit during that short time being estimated at the princely amount of £3 1s. 4d. Mr. Elgar was the first manager, Mr Dibley the film operator, Mr Barnard the door keeper and Miss Pelfrey the cashier. There were twenty two rows of seats and admission prices ranged from 3d. to 1s. 6d. Usherettes wore black dresses with white aprons and butterfly caps and received a dress allowance of 1s. 0d. per week. In April 1914 Harry B. Wincote took over the managership at a weekly wage of £2. 10s. 0d. including commission. The finances of the cinema were much affected over the ensuing years with the onset of the First World War and the loss of many of its patrons as they donned khaki. In 1915 the directors even obtained insurance against the risk from aircraft or bombardment! Losses in the first few operating years were gradually made up, although the shareholders had to be content with no dividends for several years.

Milford had been a sleepy village whose inhabitants were mainly connected with the land and no doubt earned "extras" during the days when smuggling was a well known occupation all along the Hampshire/Dorset coastline. The fortunes of Milford were closely interwoven with the owners of Newland Manor, the estate comprising 2000 acres in 1886 and owned by Col. Cornwallis-West. Through his friendship with the Duke of Devonshire, who was at that time developing Eastbourne into a fashionable resort, he tried to model Milford on those lines. Seven new roads were to be constructed, along with a new hotel, pier, bandstand, esplanade, hydropathic establishment and pleasure gardens. Only the roads, hotel and pleasure gardens were constructed, the scheme failing due to lack of capital and support, an outbreak of typhoid at a boys school in the village keeping prospective purchasers away. Thus, Milford was spared a major development and continued its uneventful course until the Edwardian heydays when Newlands Manor became one of the centres of "High Society". Here visiting Royalty created an avenue of trees which they ceremonially planted. The occasional rusty metal labels beside some of these trees and road names such as Pless, Westminster and Cornwallis are nostalgic reminders of this bygone era.

Keyhaven was a community, consisting mainly of members of several families who had connections with the sea, the "Gun" Inn being the focal point of the hamlet. Hurst Castle was still garrisoned at the turn of the century and the local postman, Harry Wills, had to walk the shingle spit to deliver the post. Likewise, in Everton the "Crown" Inn provided a central point for the small community. The local estates of Efford Park (home of Sir Beethom Whitehead) and Newlands Manor were the major influences on the hamlet.

Pennington covered an area going down to the marshes and up almost to the Forest and consisted of numerous small developments with the major development around the Church. A 13th Century chapel once existed here, the present building being Victorian.

Many of the photographs in this book are the products of well known local photographers; Frederick James Arnott, Cecil H. Elgar, Frederick W. G. Drew, Albert Edward Woodford and Willsteed of Southampton. Arnott arrived in Lymington in 1900 and commenced business at 120, High Street. He travelled the New Forest extensively, providing a comprehensive pictorial record of the local villages. In contrast to this, Elgar, whose studios were in Gosport Street, issued only a few fine views of Lymington and Milford. F. Drew took over Arnott's business in the 1920s when Arnott retired and continued business right up to the early 1950s. A. E. Woodford became well known in the area as he would cycle round with his own camera to record the local scenes. Willsteed of Southampton was one of the most prolific photographers of South Hampshire, but his fixing procedures were poor and the majority of his photographs have faded since they were taken at the turn of the century. It is fortunate that these photographers took such care in providing us with a pictorial record of our villages. Without them, this book would not have been possible.

LYMINGTON POST OFFICE c. 1910.

ACKNOWLEDGEMENTS

I am very grateful to the many people who have given me encouragement and support, loaned material, recollected bygone days and proof-read my first draft. I would especially like to thank the following people: Miss M. Berry, Mrs I. Bungay, Mr R. Coles, Mr & Mrs S. Hobby, Mr R. Jennings, Mr & Mrs D. Jenvey, Mrs O. Leyland-Jones, Miss M. L. Lewitt, Mr A. T. Lloyd, Mr & Mrs G. Munden, Mr M. Reed, Mr R. Smith, Mr I. Stevenson, Mr & Mrs C. Westwood, Mr & Mrs J. B. Young and the late Miss H. Bruce, Mr M. Cole, Mr R. Fuggett, Mr W. Hackwell, Mr C. Saunders, Mr T. E. Stone and Mrs O. Troke. Special thanks go to Miss R. Young who by continual persistence actually forced me to put pen to paper and who has spent hours correcting my grammar and typing the manuscript.

Bibliography: *The Story of Lymington*, R. Coles; *A Walk through Lymington*, E. King; *Lymington High Street Then and Now*, R. Coles; *Perfect Darling*, E. Quelch; *Lymington and the New Forest Transport History*, R. Coles; Milford-on-Sea Record Society Occasional Magazines; *Lymington in Old Picture Postcards*, B. Down; *Kelly's Directory of Hampshire*, 1895; *The Salterns of the Lymington Area*, A. T. Lloyd; *Country House History*, B. Pinnell.

This book is dedicated to my parents—"A dream come true".

CONTENTS

	Page
Lymington	6-50
Pennington	51-54
Everton	55-56
Keyhaven	57-62
Milford-on-Sea	63-96

HIGH STREET c 1905. There were few worries about traffic congestion when this photograph of the High Street was taken. Besides the delivery carts, Landaus of the gentry and the horse rider, other means of transport were few and far between.

CORONATION DECORATIONS 1910. On 9th May, 1910, Mr E. F. Chinery, the mayor, proclaimed George V to be the new King from the balcony of the Angel Hotel. After the proclamation the crowds sang "God Save The King" accompanied by the Town Provincial Band. The High Street and St Thomas' Street were a blaze of colour with large strings of bunting and decorations. Following a procession and service on Coronation day, the High Street was illuminated in the evening as the festivities continued.

BAPTIST CHURCH c 1918. The Baptist Community was formally recognised in Lymington in 1689 and were known as "The Dippers" because of their practice of total immersion which they carried out in Hatchett Pond in all seasons. The church moved to its present site in New Street in 1769; the original building was demolished and the present one opened in 1835. The Reverend Henry Tree pictured here was minister from 1916-1927.

"ANCHOR AND HOPE" FIRE 1905. This was all that remained of one of Lymington's oldest public houses. In coaching days, the "Telegraph" left here daily at 5 a.m. on its journey to London, and this Inn was a stopping place for the Commercial Coach from the "Star" Hotel, Southampton, on its way to Weymouth. The fire caused great consternation, for many thought it would lead to the destruction of the whole town.

THE GROVE c. 1905. The Grove Gardens ran up towards Ashley Lane. New houses were built on the right of The Grove just before the Second World War.

LONDESBOROUGH HOTEL c. 1912. This was originally a coaching inn, later catering for motorised transport when it came into circulation and the Wilts and Dorset garages were built onto the back of the Hotel. Loader's toy and fancy goods shop can be seen to the left of the Hotel.

GENERAL ELECTION 1910. Frank Perkins was elected Unionist MP for the New Forest Division by a majority of 2093. When his victory was announced in Lymington by Mr H. Nicoll, the High Sheriff, hats were thrown, handkerchiefs waved and for five minutes a seething crowd massed outside the Angel Hotel cheering. Mr Perkins was given a magnificent reception on his arrival at Lymington.

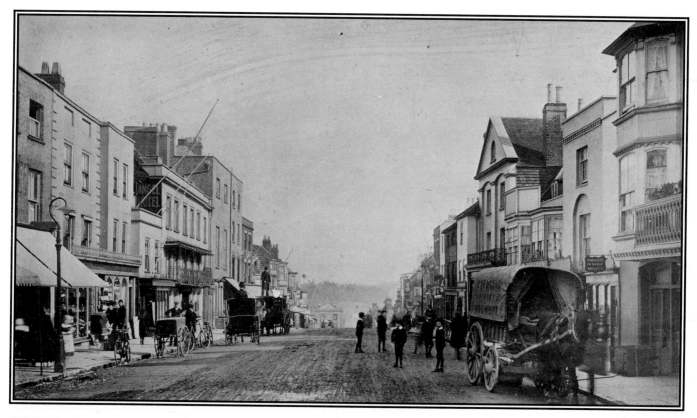

KING'S BOOKSHOP c. 1900. In 1735 John King founded a printing works in Yeovil where he made paper from rags because cheap woodpulp was unavailable. His son Charles worked as a bookseller in Dorchester before he moved to Lymington in 1805 to set up the business. In 1858 the shop moved to its present site at 105/106, High Street and Edward King took over the business from his father. Both Edward and his son Charles, who managed the business from 1914, were mayors of Lymington.

13

EMPIRE DAY AT LYMINGTON.

EMPIRE DAY c. 1907. Empire Day was a very special day for children as the ordinary lessons of the morning were replaced with patriotic lessons and addresses. In the afternoon all the children assembled in the station yard with the members of the Town Prize Band, Coastguard Men and the Cadet Corps for the march up to the Cricket Field where they were addressed by the Mayor.

EMPIRE DAY c. 1909. After the Mayor's address a lengthy programme of sports took place after which prizes were presented to the winners. At the end of all the events buns and oranges were distributed to all the children whilst an evening dance was arranged for the adults.

SNOWSTORM 1908. Memories of the terrible snowstorms of January and February 1881 were evoked when the South Coast once again experienced large snow falls.

BAND OF HOPE PROCESSION. JULY 19. 1905.

HIGH STREET. LYMINGTON.

BAND OF HOPE c. 1905. To belong to the Band of Hope you had to sign the pledge against alcohol. They would meet once a week for hymns and prayers, songs and poetry.

TOWN HALL c. 1920. The Town Hall was built in 1913 and is bordered by Plumbly's, which was a high class family grocer, and Fletcher's the butchers. From the balcony of the Town Hall the reading of proclamations took place, superseding the use of the "Angel" from which the accession of George V was proclaimed in 1910. The Town Hall was in use until 1966 when the present one in the Avenue was opened, the original site being cleared for the Earley Court shopping precinct.

18

AERIAL VIEW c. 1930. In the mid 1920s the Aerofilm Company photographed the area and this photograph is one of many issued for the town. This view shows the Lower High Street (running from left towards right) where it meets Gosport Street/Captains Row (running diagonally from top left to bottom right). In the top right hand corner the tollgate can be seen and the station a little below it.

GOSPORT STREET c. 1905. W. H. Moger's second hand furniture shop at No. 1 High Street can be seen in the centre of the picture. It is said that this was the first house in Lymington to be lit by an electric light. Ernie Markwell owned part of the grocer's seen halfway down the terraces on the left of the picture. The other grocers in the town in the 1920s were Plumbly, Rowland Hill, Willis, Markwell and International.

SOUTH STREET c. 1905. South Street consisted mainly of residences connected with river employment. The Baptists worshipped in a house in South Street in 1689 and when they moved to New Street this house became a carpenter's shop. At the turn of the century Keeping's Garage had a workshop in South Street, which is now called Captain's Row.

THE BATHS c. 1910. Here many young Lymingtonians took their first swimming lessons. The Bath House was built by the Lymington Bath and Improvement Company in 1833 and remains one of the largest sea baths in the country.

THE QUAY c. 1905. The numbers of large transport ships were greatly reduced once Lymington ceased to be a major salt producing area. However, coal and wood ships from the North still frequented the port supplying timber to Travis Arnold and coal to Clement and Rickman. This view of the Quay is taken from the railway line.

QUAY HILL c. 1910. This used to be a poorer area to live in and housed fishermen and people employed on the boats. The pathway was flagged and stoned and at one time boasted six or seven public houses within the vicinity of the Quay.

HARBOUR 1908. Another view of the harbour; this time the quayside is taken up with smaller vessels, one of these the "Marquis of Lorne" working out of Poole. As evidenced by the ice floes this may well have been the same freeze-up as seen on page 16.

BIRD'S EYE VIEW c. 1907. This view of Walhampton shows the route taken by a 14 ft rowing boat from the Quay to the old ferry house, seen here in the middle of the picture. The full journey cost a penny but the majority of clients paid a halfpenny which took them to the jetty behind the railway bridge.

WALHAMPTON HOUSE, LYMINGTON.

WALHAMPTON HOUSE c. 1905. At this time, Walhampton House was a private house owned by Viscountess St Cyres. Her Ladyship's visits to London provided a source of great interest for the local children as a special train was hired for the event. Walhampton House became a Preparatory School in the 1950s.

PRIMROSE LEAGUE c. 1908. In 1874 Pylewell House was bought by William Ingham Whitaker for £72,000. Subsequent generations of Whitakers proved to be great benefactors to the town of Lymington with the house and grounds being used for numerous functions including the Primrose League pictured here. The Primrose League was founded in 1883, its aims being the maintenance of religion, the estates of the Realm, and the unity and ascendancy of the Empire.

THE PIER c. 1925. The first crossing from Lymington to Yarmouth was made in 1830 by the 16 h.p. wooden hulled steamer "Glasgow". She weighed 51 tons and was clinker built in 1828 by Stephen Wood. Three enterprising Lymington businessmen, Charles and Samuel St. Barbe and Edward Hicks, owned the "Glasgow". The ferries now carry around 1,350,000 passengers a year.

FLOODS AT WATERLOO ROAD 1909. These floods were a regular occurrence when the river broke over the Toll Gate Sluices. Clement's coalyard in the railway station could often be badly affected. In October 1909 the floods were worse than usual and resulted in the drowning of some pigs and poultry kept by the railwaymen near the line.

CRIMEAN CANNON c. 1905. The Cannon was situated at the junction of New Street and East Hill before its disappearance around the time of the Second World War. The children pictured here from left to right are D. Jenvey, C. Morris, G. Jenvey, J. Jenvey, O. Francis, B. Jenvey, F. Jenvey and the sister of O. Francis.

PASSFORD FARM c. 1904. This farm was owned a few years later by Mr Just who used part of the farm buildings as a cattery.

LYMINGTON & DISTRICT HOSPITAL.

LYMINGTON AND DISTRICT HOSPITAL c. 1925. The hospital was built as a memorial to Edward VII, funds being obtained by public subscription. One enterprising young boy even strapped collecting boxes to his dog! The hospital consisted of two four-bedded wards, an emergency ward, operating theatre, X-ray department, dispensary and kitchen. A matron, sister and kitchen maid were employed with administration being provided by a voluntary committee.

by Lady Speyer, April 1913

OPENING OF HOSPITAL 1913. By 1930 the first of many subsequent alterations had been completed to accommodate the increasing number of patients. A children's ward was opened together with a private block and the nurses' home. A new theatre was also constructed together with physiotherapy rooms.

HOSPITAL SUNDAY PROCESSION. LYMINGTON. 1906

HOSPITAL SUNDAY PROCESSION c. 1906. This procession would begin at the railway station and go up St Thomas's Street and Queen Street before being disbanded at the Cricket Ground. Money was collected during the procession and so that the people watching from the upstairs windows of their houses should not be missed out a tube on a pole was held up and their pennies collected in a bag at the end of the tube.

LYMINGTON FIRE BRIGADE c. 1904. The two horses that pulled the fire engine were stabled behind "The Angel" and on hearing the fire bell, one would be ridden at a gallop up the High Street. The other, however, was so well trained that it would just be let loose and could be guaranteed to make its way through "The Tins", arriving at the Sports Ground before its partner.

SOUTHAMPTON BUILDINGS c. 1905. The General shop was run by Mr Ingelfield. The Cabinet and Carpenter's remained when Mr Harding took over from Mr Pardy although it ceased to be an undertakers. In 1932 these buildings were redeveloped.

WELLWORTHY'S c. 1940. Probably nothing has affected the town and the surrounding area more this century in terms of employment than the development of Wellworthy's engineering works. The Works were founded in 1919 by John Howlett, who managed South Coast Garages. The firm became justly famous for its range of piston rings.

FLOWER SHOW c. 1908. A must in the social calendar for Lymingtonians was the annual Flower Show, held in the fields at Highfield. Much effort went into the entries, as this photograph of the Decorated Mail Cart for Cottagers shows.

QUEEN STREET c. 1906. Furber's, the blacksmith, and Newman's bakery can be seen in this picture. The Anglesea Temperance Hotel opposite was owned by Harry Clifton, alcohol of course being banned from the premises. The five cottages just before the Round House had to be demolished in 1932 under the Slum Clearance Act at a cost of £750.

DRINKING FOUNTAIN c. 1907. This was situated in St Thomas's Street until it was moved between the two World Wars. The shops you can see from left to right are Hapgood, the shoe shop, Coghlan, the dentist, Priestland, the dairy, Eveleigh, the butcher, Westwood, the ironmonger, Cox the sweet shop and Arnold's garage which later became Keeping's.

WESTWOOD'S HOUSEHOLD SUPPLIES c. 1905. William Westwood was a tallow man from East Street in Southampton. He opened the Ironmongery in 1892 and sold rush baskets, besoms, heath brooms, crock jars for pickles and tin trunks for people travelling abroad, in additon to his candles, lamps and paraffin. William made his deliveries by tricycle when no longer able to use his horse and trap. The grocery was opened in 1925.

THE BUTCHER'S c. 1920. Pictured outside his butcher's shop at 18 St Thomas's Street is Mr Rowland Nappin and his daughter Ivy. Having taken over the pork butcher business from Mr Harper in 1916, Mr Nappin continued the pork butchery before becoming a general butcher. Home made brawns were a speciality costing 1s 6d. each. In 1924 he sold the business to Miss Rolls who used the premises as a private residence before it became a chemist's.

ST THOMAS' STREET c 1907. Jenvey's, later House the Bakers, can be seen as the road heads towards Priestlands Place. The local shops used to remain open until the second showing at the Lyric had finished at 9 pm as many people would come in for their week's provisions after seeing the film.

MARSHALL'S GENERAL STORE c 1910. Polly Marshall is pictured here together with her father. She sold groceries and walnuts in season, picked from a tree growing behind the shop. These walnuts would appear in a large wooden bowl on the counter and cost sixpence a pound.

TAILOR'S SHOP c. 1930. The tailoring firm of Jenvey moved from Queen Street in 1904 to No. 9 St Thomas' Street, formerly an Ironmongery owned by Mr J. Light, and soon became one of the largest bespoke tailors along the South Coast. Don Jenvey and Eddie Goff are pictured here outside the shop.

WORKFORCE OF JENVEY'S 1912. The workforce of Jenvey's is pictured in the cutter's room at the back of the shop. The staff amounted to fourteen including John Jenvey the founder of the tailoring business. The back row of the picture shows G. Jenvey, J. Jenvey, C. Rogers, G. Haller and F. Knight. Pictured on the front row are; B. Knight, R. Munden, G. Kennedy, E. Jenvey and M. Rowe.

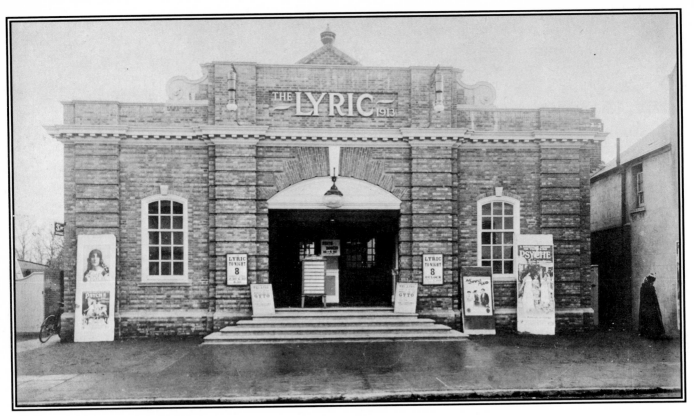

THE LYRIC c. 1913. The children's matinees on a Saturday afternoon cost three half pennies and were very disorderly with orange peel being thrown and little respect being shown for the King at the end of a performance! There were three houses on a Saturday, the last finishing at eleven o'clock.

CANON MATURIN'S FUNERAL 1905. The venerable vicar of Lymington, Canon Maturin, died in November 1905. He was a curate of Ringwood Parish in his earlier years, moving to Lymington when he was in his late thirties. He was an eloquent preacher and read the lessons fluently without his glasses. He was to remain in Lymington for 53 years until his sudden death at the grand age of 89 years.

WOODSIDE c. 1905. This shows a residential house with a small shop on the right, which was run by Mrs. Harder. Some of the houses were demolished when the road was widened.

THE BLACKSMITH'S c. 1908. This view of Pennington Crossroads shows Mr Anderson the blacksmith in the centre. Carthorses used for pulling the drays had to have their shoes renewed every six weeks as the granite in the metalled roads quickly wore them down; as a consequence a blacksmith was never short of work. The smithy closed in the 1930s and nothing remains of these buildings today.

POST OFFICE c. 1908. In 1895 William Francis Aldin was sub-postmaster of Pennington Post Office. Letters arriving through Lymington at 6.15 am and 12.30 pm were dispatched from Pennington at 12.30 and 6.15 pm. Mr Hayter was the sub-postmaster in 1908.

PENNINGTON VILLAGE c. 1908. The camera proved to be a great source of interest to these local children in North Street. In the background can be seen the "Lion and Lamb" public house (now The "Musketeers"), George Dyer being "mine host" at the turn of the century.

MILK DELIVERIES c. 1920. Pictured is Joseph William Smith's milk float at Saddler's Farm in Lower Pennington where the family have farmed for over 100 years. Before becoming a tenant farmer Mr. Smith had been the Landlord of the "Chequers" Inn in Woodside. All dairy farms had their own milk rounds and there was always keen competition to gain new clients, milk costing about 2½d. a pint. There were usually two rounds a day and it was not unknown for less scrupulous farmers to water down their milk when the cows were not yielding sufficient to meet their orders.

"CROWN INN" c. 1910. The Everton Club's fete was held at the "Crown" Inn on Whit Monday and was a general holiday for the district. The club members and most of the village people processed behind the village band and a man who carried a heavy, heart-shaped garland of flowers. The processions ended at the local gentry's homes where refreshments were available. In the forecourt would be a coconut shy and stalls selling novelties and food.

EVERTON VILLAGE c. 1908. On the right hand side of the crossroads can be seen the former Methodist Chapel, which has since been demolished. This was the site of the village pound where animals found straying on the highway would be kept. They were fed and watered by the local people.

MEAD'S STORES c. 1920. Charles Mead is pictured here with his son, Charles, and daughter, Nora. He opened his grocery shop in 1916 and in so doing, began a family business that was to continue for the next sixty four years, expanding in later years to include the sub Post Office.

THE GUN c. 1900. The landlord of "The Gun" at this time was Arthur Payne, pictured in the middle foreground. Arthur was also the Harbour Master and was famous in the hamlet for his act of rowing the Prince of Wales, later Edward VII, down the river. The house next to "The Gun" was named "Hawker's Cottage" after Colonel Hawker who, it is said, founded the sport of wild fowling.

PRUDE'S COTTAGE c. 1905. The Prude family were fishermen and wild-fowlers and on clear frosty nights it was a common occurrence to find them out on Oxey lake in pursuit of widgeon and other wildfowl feeding on the mud flats. The guns they used were the size of a small drainpipe and consequently had to be brought ashore to be loaded.

OLD TOLL GATE c. 1905. The Toll Gate was situated on the ancient road to Lower Pennington. In the distance "Harewood House" can be seen. This house, reputed to be haunted, suffered a serious fire, and remained empty for many years before being demolished.

FRANK SHUTTLER c. 1905. Frank was the last man to convey supplies to the coastguard and lighthouse keepers at Hurst Castle. He can be seen here, complete with wheelbarrow and sacks, about to depart from the Quay for the Castle. Behind him is the Post Office and in the far right of the picture is situated the Coastguard Station which has since been superseded by the facilities at Calshot.

HMS GLADIATOR 1908. This terrible disaster occurred in the Solent during a blinding snowstorm on the afternoon of Saturday 25th April. An American liner, St. Paul, outward bound from Southampton to New York rammed HMS Gladiator which was so badly damaged that it capsized. Twenty-seven people on the Gladiator lost their lives in this tragedy. After many months the ship was righted and towed to Portsmouth for repair.

THE VILLAGE c. 1905. This lane approached Milford from Hordle Cliff and is bordered by the Water Meadows on its left hand side. These meadows took the overflow of the Dane Stream and were once a mass of marsh marigolds and yellow flags.

POOR HOUSE c. 1905. The Poor House on the right of the picture was part of the Lymington Union. In later years it was destined to become Lloyds Bank. The bank later moved to purpose built premises on the opposite side of the road. In the distance are Keeping's Garage, Hames' Tea Rooms and Woodman and Swan, the dressmakers.

KEEPING'S GARAGE c. 1930. The Garage was founded by Fred Keeping in 1895 and Frank Keeping assumed management of the Milford business in 1921 upon his return from the Armed Forces. One of the features of the Keeping Service in those earlier days was its taxi service which managed to function throughout both World Wars. Pictured here from left to right are: R. Parker, J. Hackwell, S. Hales, B. Hobby, L. White, J. Keeping and S. Hobby (author's father).

MILFORD TEA ROOMS c. 1925. The tea rooms were owned by Mrs. Hames, who kept a parrot in the window. She also sold groceries and toys and at Christmas they created a grotto which cost two pence to see. This grotto was marvellous for children as it consisted of large caves with little trains running round.

BASKET INDUSTRY c. 1925. The Basket Factory was located behind Mrs. Hames' Sweet Shop and started around 1920. The workforce was split into two sheds, one for men, who made the larger wicker items and the other for women. Their products were retailed in Weymouth, Wimborne and Bournemouth, a wastepaper bin selling for 1s. 6d. The wages were five shillings a week and M. Berry is seen here making a cycle basket.

THE BAKEHOUSE c. 1920. Tom Miles worked in the bakehouse and it is said that he baked very good bread in spite of the black beetles and weevils that sometimes appeared in his loaves. The War Memorial on the side of the bakehouse commemorates the village men who went to the First World War and those who were never to return. The bakehouse was demolished in the early 1930s and was replaced by a mock Tudor building that later became a wine shop.

A DAY'S OUTING c. 1925. It was commonplace around this time to hire a charabanc for a day's outing. It is pictured here in Milford, probably at the start of a Baptist Church outing.

RED LION c. 1905. One day, some men from Hurst refused to leave at closing time so George Barnes, the landlord, fetched a hive of bees from the garden and threw it into the bar. It was cleared in no time at all! In the early 1900s children used to sit amongst the chimneys of the "Red Lion" and throw berries at unsuspecting drunkards wending their way along the pavements.

RICKMAN'S TEA ROOMS c. 1925. More affectionately known as Dolly's Sweet Shop, this was a favourite shop for the local schoolchildren and the choirboys on their paynights, when they would rush down for hot Vimto or peppermint drinks, crisps and biscuits. During the summer ice-cream, lemonade and mineral waters were sold. Mrs George Rickman is pictured outside the shop with her son Arthur.

VILLAGE CENTRE c. 1905. The chickens pictured here in front of the Smithy belonged to George Miles who owned the butchers shop on the left hand side of the picture. The football team used to pin their notices for the week on the large oak tree next to the butchers shop.

KNIGHT'S GENERAL STORE c. 1925. C. L. Knight bought the Sweet Shop in 1912 and the grocery shop after the war. The two shops were combined, each shop having its own entrance. Handmade sweets and ice-cream were sold and teas were served on the lawn. Knight's also supplied the catering for cricket matches held at Newlands Manor. In 1933 the grocery shop was transferred up Church Hill and the original grocery became an off-licence.

HIGH STREET c. 1905. Frederick Pascall, manager of George Miles' butcher's shop, can be seen in the foreground. Pickled tongues were his speciality and he always had calves heads and sweetbreads to hand.

AERIAL VIEW c. 1925. This view is interesting as it shows the large area of parkland belonging to Milford House in the top right of the picture. This parkland became famous with its mention in an edition of "Punch" concerning a printing error that appeared in the "Lymington Times"—"the coronation will be held on Milford lawn by kind permission of Mr. Agar". "Punch" commented "not at Westminster as we had expected".

ALL SAINTS' PARISH CHURCH c. 1905. The Church dates back to the eleventh century. Around 1910 there was a fear that Suffragettes might damage the church. It was decided to keep a continual watch. One enthusiastic watcher found a suspicious parcel in the choir stalls and felt sure it was a bomb. She bravely placed it in a bucket of water outside only to find that it contained twelve new hymn books!

ANCIENT ORDER OF FORESTERS c. 1900. The Milford-on-Sea Court Goodwyn was founded in 1883 and they used to hold fetes in the field where the new vicarage now stands. Before the onset of the National Health Service members would be entitled to medical attention and free medicine plus a weekly allowance providing they paid a weekly subscription of 6d, or 2d for those over 70 years old.

MILFORD BAND c. 1900. The band was started by the vicar Mr Wilkinson who bought the instruments for £80 and it continued until his death in 1908, when the band came to an end as so few attended practices. Pictured here on the back row are G. Berry, T. Pike, R. Whatley, W. Hackwell, L. Rooke (bandmaster), F. Pike, W. Nicklen and T. Jury. On the front row are: C. Church, J. Goodridge, F. Golden, H. Troke and S. Stride.

NEWLANDS MANOR. Newlands Manor was at its heyday at the turn of the century when the Prince of Wales (later King Edward VII) was a regular visitor to the Colonel and Mrs Cornwallis-West's home. The Lymington 4th Vol. Battn. Hampshire Regt. band used to play on the lawn for the royal visitor. One day Mrs West jokingly told the Prince that she called them her band, to which he replied, "But they are wearing my uniform!"

THE CROSSROADS c. 1904. Bread and confectionery was sold from one side of these premises, the other side being a pork butcher's. A large bakehouse was built on at the rear and this extension was made very up to date by the addition of a chute from the chaff cutter down to bins for the horses to feed. In later years, one side of this bakehouse was to become a gentlemen's hairdresser's owned by Tablow Day.

MOORE'S GARAGE c. 1945. By the late 1940s Moore's had developed into this impressive building, long outgrowing the little shed in which Fred Moore and Ted Pragnell had started the business in 1918, repairing cars and bicycles. Petrol supplies came from Lymington Quay in two gallon cans and were delivered by horse and cart. In the foreground, the street lamp, affectionately known as the "George and Mary", commemorates their Coronation in 1910.

WILTS AND DORSET BANK c. 1900. This view shows the Wilts and Dorset bank followed by the Post Office. Cottons and silks were sold from the thatched cottage next to the Milford Cycle Works which were owned by F. Keeping. The thatched cottage was demolished shortly after the turn of the century and a Working Men's Club built in its place.

POSTCART c. 1900. The Post Office was originally a haphazard affair with the letters being placed in Louisa Cole's window to await collection. Around the turn of the century, it moved to the site shown here with the postman and local telegraph boy (W. Hobby, my grandfather) on board the post cart. The Post Office did not remain on this site for long and by 1910 it had moved to its present site by the Old Smithy.

The Village, Milford-on-Sea

STONE'S THE PRINTERS c. 1920. In 1920 Telford and Gwen Stone started their stationery shop in the High Street. They ran a printing business with one treadle-press on which they turned out posters, billheads, meat tickets and even hard-back books!

84

HIGH STREET c. 1905. This view of the eastern end of the High Street shows the remnants of a Hospital Sunday parade. Many of the houses on the left hand side have since been turned into shops, their gardens becoming pavements.

METHODIST DEDICATION c. 1910. In 1901 Mr Cove was invited to be minister of the Baptist Church and he remained here until a dispute occurred concerning the admission of Christians of other denominations. This led to the resignation of Mr Cove and, together with other dissatisfied members of the Church, they retreated to the back of Spreadbury's until the Methodist Church could be built.

COTTAGE HOSPITAL c. 1908. The hospital was built as a result of a nasty accident that occurred in Keyhaven. A man fell off a rick and was so badly hurt that he had to be taken to Boscombe hospital on a farm cart, there being no hospital nearer. Dr. Bruce was so concerned about this that he approached Mr Agar of Milford House about the lack of nearby hospitals. A plot of land was chosen and the Cottage Hospital was built.

SMALLEST HOUSE c. 1925. Alice James and Jessie Rose are pictured here outside the smallest house in the village; it consisted of two rooms and belonged to Harry Vickers. It is said the house was sparsely furnished with orange boxes for chairs. Young boys from the village enjoyed climbing onto the roof and putting a slate over the chimney pot to smoke out Mr. Vickers. The house was completely demolished around 1927.

KEYHAVEN ROAD c. 1905. This picture shows Neal's Terrace on the right and Carrington Terrace on the left. The house on the far left hand side was once an ale house with skittle alley.

THE LAUNDRY c. 1915. The laundry was opened in 1896 by Madame Paulina Patti who was a maid to Mrs Cornwallis-West. It then cost you two pence to have your drawers washed, a penny for collars and cuffs, and stockings were a penny a pair! There were reductions for servants at ½d per item. It was destroyed by fire in 1898 but was rebuilt and was in operation until it finally closed in 1973.

THE WHITE HOUSE.
MILFORD-ON-SEA.

THE WHITE HOUSE c. 1905. Walker Munro from Rhinefield had The White House built as his summer residence. He designed the House like the bridge of a ship, port hole windows included. On the seaward side, there were two derricks for the lowering of rowing boats into the sea. Many village fetes and pageants were held here.

ON PARADE c. 1915. The Indians are pictured here outside Christie's shop, which sold fancy goods, crested china and a great variety of pictorial postcards. The Post Office is seen next door followed by the Old Smithy which was owned by Mr Quelch who sold bicycles and bath chairs. The Indians' stay was of short duration for in February 1916, the last of them had returned to the war front.

CONVALESCENT INDIAN TROOPS c. 1915. 787 Indian soldiers stayed in the village during the period of the Occupation. An enterprising film company took advantage of this situation and made a film of the troops which was shown in cinemas of this era. The eastern part of High Street became an Indian bazaar whilst other scenes saw the soldiers scaling the cliffs.

HOTEL VICTORIA c. 1910. This hotel was built as part of the aborted primary development when Milford was going to become another Eastbourne. It was the headquarters of the convalescent Indian troops during the First World War. Changing its name in later years to become the Solent Court Hotel before being demolished in the 1960s, the area lost a fine old building when the developers moved in.

VICTORIA HALL AND CLUB c. 1915. The Hall was built by public subscription for Queen Victoria's Diamond Jubilee and was used for entertainment purposes including the showing of films, badminton, small bore rifle shooting, dancing and concert performances. The Hall was built on the site of some cart sheds that were used for hiding contraband on the smuggling route from Frog Lane, via Barnes Lane to the Forest. It was later converted to a Roman Catholic Church.

VINEGAR HILL c. 1905. Going from right to left, the buildings are Hillside House, once a former malthouse, Pike's workshop, Hillside Cottages and Rose Cottage outside which several of the convalescent Indians came to grief against the wall as they failed to negotiate the bend on their bicycles. The occupants of Hillside Cottages were well practised at tending to their injuries. Hillside House and Pike's workshop have since been demolished and the name "Vinegar Hill" transferred.